CHRISTMAS COOKING

Holiday Recipes,

Menus and Gifts

BY BIBB JORDAN

Peachtree Publishers, Ltd.

Published by
PEACHTREE PUBLISHERS, LTD.
494 Armour Circle, NE
Atlanta, Georgia 30324

Manufactured in the United States of America

10 9 8 7 6 5 4 3 2 1

Library of Congress Catalog Card Number 87-80968

ISBN 0-934601-33-X

For The Christmas Children

Patrick, April,
Allen, Eliot,
Chris, Cheyenne,
Warren, Tom,
Katharine, Alison,
Caitlin
and Tyler

TABLE OF CONTENTS

One   Hors D'Oeuvres 1

Two   Gifts 11

Three   Christmas Cookies 21

Four   Desserts 29

Five   Christmas Open House, Menu for 20-25 39

Six   Christmas Eve Supper, Menu for 8 51

Seven   Elegant Christmas Day Dinner, Menu for 8 55

Eight   Index 64

ONE

HORS D'OEUVRES

*Chutney Almond Cheese Mold**
*Crab Mousse**
*Macadamia Cheddar Snaps**
*Hot Olive Onion Triangles**
*Honey Raisin Meatballs in Chafing Dish**
*Curried Chicken on Bibb Boats**
Maple Butter Ham Canapes
*Shrimp Mousse**
Hot Spicy Oysters on Croutons

* *A make-ahead recipe*

The recipes presented here can be enjoyed almost any time of the year, but because of such ingredients as honey, maple syrup, raisins, and lots of good sharp cheddar and curry, they're particularly nice to serve to guests at Christmas. The Chutney Almond Cheese Mold and Macadamia Cheddar Snaps are fairly easy and can be made well ahead and brought out for unexpected company during the holidays. Both Maple Butter Ham Canapes and Curried Chicken on Bibb Boats are unique and fun and a pleasant change from the ubiquitous cheese and crackers and crudités with dip. And if you're an oyster lover, don't miss the Hot Spicy Oysters on buttery rounds of toasted French bread.

CHUTNEY ALMOND CHEESE MOLD

16 ounces cream cheese, softened
2 cups sharp cheddar cheese, grated
6 tablespoons sherry
2 tablespoons Worcestershire sauce
1½ teaspoons curry
½ teaspoon salt
1 8-ounce jar Major Grey's Chutney
¾ cup almonds, toasted, coarsely chopped
½ cup green onions, thinly sliced
½ cup coconut, flaked

Combine cream cheese, cheddar, sherry, Worcestershire, curry and salt until well blended. Pour into a mold that has been lined with plastic wrap. Wrap well with additional plastic wrap or aluminum foil. Freeze for several hours or overnight. Unmold and spread with chutney. Press the chopped almonds on top, followed by a layer of green onions and a layer of coconut. (The mold may be frozen as much as a week ahead of time; bring out of the freezer at least one hour before serving, then garnish and let it remain at room temperature.) Serves 10 to 12, or more if part of a cocktail buffet.

CRAB MOUSSE

1 4-cup mold
Vegetable oil
¼ cup, plus 1 tablespoon homemade
mayonnaise (see page 41)
1½ teaspoons fresh lime juice
1½ teaspoons fresh lemon juice
1 tablespoon fresh parsley, chopped
1 tablespoon green onion, finely
chopped
¼ teaspoon Tabasco
1¼ teaspoons salt
¼ teaspoon white pepper
1 tablespoon Knox unflavored
gelatin
2 tablespoons cold water
1 pound fresh lump crabmeat
¾ cup cream, whipped

Prepare a 4-cup mold by oiling lightly with vegetable oil. Place several ice cubes in the mold and add enough water to fill to the top. Set aside to chill while finishing recipe.

Mix mayonnaise, lime and lemon juice, parsley, onion, Tabasco, salt and pepper. Set aside. Place gelatin in the 2 tablespoons cold water, soften, then dissolve over hot boiling water. Cool slightly, then combine with the mayonnaise mixture. Carefully fold in the crabmeat. Whip cream, and fold into crab mixture — work lightly but thoroughly. Taste for seasoning, adding more lemon juice or Tabasco if needed.

Pour ice and water from mold; tap mold against sink or counter to remove excess moisture. Pour mousse into the prepared mold, and chill about 5 hours or until set. Garnish with finely chopped fresh herbs (such as basil, tarragon or chives), or create a design with red caviar and finely chopped black olives. Keep refrigerated until ready to serve. (The mousse may be made the day before, unmolded and garnished right before serving.) Serves 10 to 12. As part of a cocktail buffet, will serve 25 to 30.

MACADAMIA CHEDDAR SNAPS

¼ cup butter, softened
1 cup Bisquik
1 egg, slightly beaten
1 cup Macadamia nuts, coarsely chopped
½ cup sharp cheddar cheese, grated
Cayenne pepper to taste

Preheat oven to 400 degrees. Blend butter and Bisquik until the mixture is in coarse crumbs. Stir in egg, nuts, cheese and cayenne pepper. Taste for seasoning, and add more cayenne if needed. Drop by the teaspoon full onto a greased cookie sheet. Bake for 8 minutes. Store in an airtight container. Makes 42 to 48.

HOT OLIVE ONION TRIANGLES

1 4½ ounce can black olives, chopped
⅓ cup green onions, diced
¾ cup cheddar cheese, grated
4 tablespoons mayonnaise
Salt
Curry powder, to taste
Freshly ground black pepper
1 small loaf Pepperidge Farm Thin-Sliced White Bread, sliced into triangles and crusts removed, toasted on just 1 side
Parsley, minced

Mix together olives, onion, cheese, mayonnaise, salt, and curry powder. Spread on untoasted side of the bread. Broil until bubbly. Sprinkle with minced parsley. Serve immediately. (The olive mixture may be prepared the day before, then spread on the toast triangles and run under the broiler just before serving.) Serves 8.

HONEY RAISIN MEATBALLS IN CHAFING DISH

¾ **pound ground sirloin**
¼ **cup onion, chopped**
¼ **cup raisins, chopped**
¼ **cup golden raisins, chopped**
2 **tablespoons green bell pepper, minced**
1 **tablespoon red bell pepper, minced**
1 **large egg, lightly beaten**
2 **tablespoons sour cream**
  Salt
  Pepper to taste

2 **tablespoons vegetable oil**
2 **teaspoons flour**
1 **cup beef stock**
¼ **cup dry red wine**
⅓ **cup red currant jelly**
¼ **cup red-wine vinegar**
3 **tablespoons honey**
3 **teaspoons tomato paste**

With your hands, combine well the first 10 ingredients, and then form into 1-inch balls. In a stainless or enameled skillet, brown the meatballs in the oil. Cook in batches, so as not to crowd and break apart the meatballs. Transfer with a slotted spoon to a plate after browning.

Pour off all but 2 teaspoons of the fat and, in the same skillet, add 2 teaspoons flour and cook the roux over moderate heat, stirring, for 30 seconds. Add beef stock, wine, jelly, vinegar, honey, and tomato paste. Cook the mixture, stirring, for 2 minutes. Return meatballs to the skillet, heat for 2 minutes, and transfer to a chafing dish to serve warm. (The meatballs can be made the day before and then gently reheated just before serving. If so, take from the refrigerator 30 minutes to 1 hour before returning to the skillet so that the mixture will reheat evenly and thoroughly.) Serves 8 to 10.

CURRIED CHICKEN ON BIBB BOATS

2 cups heavy cream
1 tablespoon curry powder
  Salt
  Freshly ground black pepper
  Pinch cayenne pepper
2 small bananas, peeled and diced
1 Granny Smith apple, peeled and diced
1 whole chicken breast, skinned, poached, boned and diced
¼ cup cashews, finely chopped and toasted
5 heads Bibb lettuce, washed, dried and separated, selecting 30 small leaves
  Green onions, washed, trimmed and very thinly sliced
  Red currants

Combine cream, curry, salt, pepper and cayenne in a heavy skillet. Cook until the mixture has been reduced by half, stirring frequently until sauce is thick. Add banana, apple and chicken and cook approximately 1 minute. (The recipe can be made the day ahead up to this point and *gently* reheated, being careful not to overcook apple and bananas.) Add cashews and check for seasoning.

Spoon about 1 tablespoon of the warm chicken curry mixture onto the crisp, dry Bibb lettuce leaves. Garnish with 3 or 4 rings of green onion and 3 or 4 tiny red currants. Makes 30.

MAPLE-BUTTER HAM CANAPES

2 cups yellow cornmeal
½ cup all-purpose flour
2 teaspoons baking powder
1 teaspoon salt
½ teaspoon baking soda
1 cup buttermilk
1 cup milk
¼ cup unsalted butter, melted
2 large eggs
½ cup unsalted butter, softened
2 tablespoons maple syrup
½ teaspoon Dijon mustard
8 thin slices lightly smoked ham
    Coarsely ground black pepper
    Watercress, rinsed and dried

Preheat oven to 450 degrees. Into a large bowl sift the cornmeal, flour, baking powder, salt and baking soda; stir. In another bowl, mix together the two milks, melted butter and eggs. Add the milk mixture to the dry ingredients and stir to combine. Pour into a 12-inch by 18-inch well buttered baking pan and bake 10 to 15 minutes, or until cornbread begins to shrink from sides of pan. Cool completely in pan. Meanwhile, combine the softened butter, maple syrup and mustard. Let stand together at room temperature while preparing cornbread rounds.

When cornbread is cool, turn onto a baking sheet. Using a serrated knife, slice horizontally to form a ⅜-inch thickness — it may be necessary to cut the sheet of bread into halves or fourths to make slicing easier. Make sure the slice is no thicker than ⅜ so the canapes will not be too bready. (Freeze any leftover cornbread in a plastic bag for later use, such as stuffing.) Spread the maple-butter mixture onto the cornbread. Cover with ham slices and refrigerate until the butter is firm (30 minutes or more). Cut out canapes using a 1½-inch round or fluted biscuit cutter. Garnish each with a generous sprinkling of freshly ground pepper and a small leaf or sprig of watercress. Makes 32 canapes.

SHRIMP MOUSSE

1 6-cup mold
  Vegetable oil, for preparing mold
8 ounces cream cheese, softened
½ cup homemade mayonnaise (see page 41)
1 cup sour cream
¼ cup green bell pepper, minced
¼ cup celery, minced
¼ cup green onion, minced
2 tablespoons red pepper, minced
¼ cup chili sauce
½ teaspoon salt
2 teaspoons Worcestershire sauce
  dash Tabasco
1 tablespoon unflavored Knox gelatin
  Juice of 1 lemon
⅛ cup cold water
3 cups shrimp, cooked, peeled, deveined and finely chopped

Prepare mold by following the same instructions for the Crab Mousse (page 3). Set aside to chill while preparing recipe.

Mix together cream cheese, mayonnaise and sour cream. Add bell pepper, celery, green onion and all other seasonings; combine thoroughly.

Dissolve gelatin in the lemon juice and ⅛ cup cold water. Heat in double boiler 5 to 10 minutes. Gradually fold gelatin into the cheese mixture. Add shrimp and blend well. Taste mixture and add more Tabasco, chili sauce or lemon juice, if needed, making sure mousse is *well* seasoned. Pour water and ice from the mold, shaking once or twice to remove excess moisture; pour the mousse mixture into the prepared mold. Cover and refrigerate overnight. Unmold and garnish with watercress, fresh dill, or finely chopped green onion. Serve with crackers. Serves 15.

HOT SPICY OYSTERS ON CROUTONS

5 tablespoons butter
1 clove garlic, minced
24 slices French bread
24 raw oysters
12 strips bacon, cut in half
12 whole water chestnuts, sliced in
half
1 jar Pickapeppa Sauce

Melt butter in skillet. Sauté garlic 2 to 3 minutes, until fragrant. Brush butter-garlic mixture on French bread and run under broiler until barely browned. Set aside.

Wrap a half strip of bacon around an oyster and a slice of water chestnut. Secure with a toothpick. Place on a shallow ovenproof serving dish. Pour Pickapeppa Sauce (this Jamaican sauce can be found in the grocery store next to Worcestershire sauce and similar condiments or in the gourmet section) over each one. Broil until bacon is cooked on one side, then turn and broil on the other side. Serve with the French garlic bread, each guest assembling his or her own hors d'oeuvre. (The oysters may be wrapped with chestnut and bacon and refrigerated for three to four hours, then covered with sauce right before broiling.) Makes 24.

TWO

GIFTS

*Brown Sugar Walnuts**
*Salted Pecans**
*Christopher's Christmas Chocolate Sauce**
*Raspberry Guava Sauce**
*Honey-Maple Mustard**
*Sweet Horseradish Mustard**
*Chocolate Orange Truffles**
*Rum-Flavored Chocolate Truffles**
*Giant Coconut Chippers**
*Candied Grapefruit Peel**

* *A make-ahead recipe*

There's nothing so special as receiving something wonderful to eat, particularly when it has been made by the hands of a good friend. And nearly all the recipes here are so simple to make that even the youngest members of the family can help with preparations. The Candied Grapefruit Peel and the mustards look beautiful in sparkling clear jars; the two nut recipes are great stocking stuffers; the truffle recipes and chocolate sauce are the *perfect* gifts for every chocoholic; and the Giant Coconut Chippers are fun presents for children. Wrap them all up with lots of ribbon curls and colorful paper, and your loved ones will thank you all year.

11

BROWN SUGAR WALNUTS

1½ cups light brown sugar
1 teaspoon light corn syrup
½ teaspoon cinnamon
    pinch ground cloves
½ cup sherry
¼ teaspoon salt
2-3 cups English walnut halves

Cook all ingredients, except walnuts, to the soft ball stage. Remove from heat and add walnuts. Stir gently and turn out on wax paper. Separate at once, using two spoons or forks. Store in airtight containers. Makes 2 dozen.

SALTED PECANS

4 tablespoons unsalted butter
1 pound shelled pecan halves
1 tablespoon salt
½ teaspoon white pepper

Preheat oven to 350 degrees. Melt butter in a shallow baking pan. Add pecans and stir well. Bake 20 minutes, stirring every 5 minutes. Remove from the oven and sprinkle with salt and pepper. Let pecans cool in pan. Store in an airtight container.

CHRISTOPHER'S CHRISTMAS CHOCOLATE SAUCE

1 cup heavy cream
6 tablespoons unsalted butter, cut in small pieces
$\frac{2}{3}$ cup granulated sugar
$\frac{2}{3}$ cup dark brown sugar, firmly packed
1 teaspoon vanilla extract
$\frac{1}{8}$ teaspoon salt
1 cup Droste cocoa powder, sifted

Cook cream and butter together in a heavy saucepan over moderate heat, stirring constantly, until the butter is melted and the cream comes to a low boil. Add sugars and vanilla, and stir for a few minutes, until sugar is dissolved. Add the salt and sifted cocoa. Reduce heat, and stir briskly with a whisk until the sauce is smooth. Pour into gift jars. When cooled, cover and store in the refrigerator. Tell gift recipients to reheat gently in a heavy saucepan or in a microwave oven (it's also good straight from the refrigerator, using a large spoon). Makes approximately 3 cups.

RASPBERRY GUAVA SAUCE

4 large oranges
4 tablespoons butter
2 (10 ounce) packages frozen
   raspberries, thawed and pureed
4 tablespoons guava paste
2 ounces raspberry liqueur
2 ounces Creme de Cassis

Remove 9 or 10 strips of peel (colored portion only) from the oranges. Juice the oranges, remove seeds and pulp, and reserve juice. In a heavy saucepan, sauté the orange peel strips in the 4 tablespoons butter about 2 minutes over low heat. Add the juice and simmer about 5 minutes. Add the pureed raspberries and the guava paste. Simmer, stirring constantly, for about 3 to 5 minutes. Stir in a small amount of water to thin the sauce. Add the liqueurs and simmer 2 to 3 minutes more. Cool and store in refrigerator. Delicious over ice cream or fruit. Makes approximately 2 cups.

HONEY-MAPLE MUSTARD

1 cup Grey Poupon Dijon mustard
4 tablespoons honey
2½ tablespoons maple syrup
¼ teaspoon allspice
¼ teaspoon ground cloves
¼ teaspoon cinnamon
1 teaspoon lemon juice
 Salt, to taste

In a glass container, combine all ingredients; mix thoroughly. Check for seasoning. Pour into a gift-sized jar. Give alone or in a small basket with other homemade mustards and sauces. This mustard is particularly good served with turkey or ham. Makes approximately 1½ cups.

SWEET HORSERADISH MUSTARD

½ cup dry mustard
½ cup white vinegar
1 egg
½ cup sugar
2 tablespoons grated horseradish, drained
2 tablespoons shallot, finely chopped
¼ teaspoon salt
⅛ teaspoon ground cloves
 Cayenne pepper, to taste

Combine the mustard and vinegar and let stand, covered, overnight.

Lightly beat the egg with the sugar. In an enamel saucepan, whisk egg and sugar together with the mustard mixture. Add remaining ingredients and cook over medium low heat until it thickens, about 10 minutes. Do not let boil. Allow mustard to cool, then pour into gift-sized jars. Store in the refrigerator. Makes approximately 1½ cups.

15

CHOCOLATE ORANGE TRUFFLES

Dutch cocoa powder, preferably
Droste
1 cup cream
3 bars bittersweet chocolate (3½
ounces each), broken in pieces
3 tablespoons unsalted butter
1 tablespoon orange rind, minced
⅓ cup confectioners' sugar
2 tablespoons orange liqueur

Cover a tray with waxed paper and dust lightly with cocoa powder. In a heavy medium saucepan, boil the cream over medium heat until reduced to ½ cup (about 10 minutes). Remove from heat. Add the chocolate to the hot cream and stir until melted (about 5 minutes). Blend in butter, orange rind, confectioners' sugar and orange liqueur. Cover and refrigerate until mixture is firm enough to handle (this may be made up to this point 1 day in advance). Shape the mixture into 1-inch balls and place on the prepared tray. Lightly dust the truffles with cocoa and chill for 20 minutes. Transfer to tiny paper cups, cover, and refrigerate.

RUM-FLAVORED CHOCOLATE TRUFFLES

16 ounces semisweet chocolate
16 tablespoons unsalted butter, softened
 6 egg yolks
 5 tablespoons dark rum
 1 teaspoon vanilla extract
¾ cup Dutch cocoa powder, preferably Droste
¾ cup confectioners' sugar

In a double boiler, melt the chocolate over simmering water. Beat in the softened butter, egg yolks, rum and vanilla with a wire whisk. Remove from heat and refrigerate until the mixture is firm enough to handle, at least 1 hour. (Truffles may be made up to this point 1 day in advance; if refrigerating longer than 1 hour, be sure to cover tightly.) Combine cocoa and confectioners' sugar. Shape the chilled chocolate mixture into 1-inch round balls, and roll in the cocoa and sugar. Store in airtight containers in the refrigerator.

GIANT COCONUT CHIPPERS

1½ cups flour
½ teaspoon salt
1 teaspoon baking soda
1 teaspoon cinnamon
12 tablespoons unsalted butter, softened
2 teaspoons vanilla extract
1 teaspoon lemon juice
⅔ cup dark brown sugar, firmly packed
⅓ cup sugar
2 eggs
½ cup coarsely chopped dates
½ cup quick cooking oats
1 cup shredded coconut
1 cup walnuts
1 cup semisweet chocolate bits

Line baking sheets with aluminum foil. Adjust racks so that 2 baking sheets can be placed in oven at the same time. Preheat oven to 350 degrees.

Sift together flour, salt, soda and cinnamon; set aside. Mix together butter, vanilla, lemon juice and sugars. Beat in eggs, one at a time. Add the chopped dates and let stand 2 or 3 minutes to soften. Add the flour mixture, mixing on low speed. Add oats. Beat just until mixed. Stir in coconut, walnuts and chocolate bits. (Before proceeding, it may help in handling to let the dough chill slightly in the refrigerator, for 15 to 20 minutes; it may also be made ahead up to this point, and the cookies baked the next day.) Using a ¼-cup measurer, form mounds of dough. Roll dough into balls; flatten to ½-inch thicknesses and place on lined baking sheets. Do not place more than 4 cookies to a baking sheet; then bake 2 sheets at a time, reversing the sheets from top to bottom to ensure even browning. Bake until well-colored, 14 to 16 minutes. Let rest about 1 minute after removing from oven — until firm enough to handle — then transfer to wire racks to cool. Makes 14 to 16 giant cookies.

CANDIED GRAPEFRUIT PEEL

2 cups grapefruit peel, cut into thin
   strips
1½ cups cold water
 ½ cup water
 1 cup sugar
   Extra sugar for coating

Place in a heavy saucepan the strips of grapefruit peel along with the 1½ cups cold water. Bring slowly to a boil and simmer 10 to 12 minutes. Drain. Repeat the simmering process 4 or 5 times, draining well each time.

Meanwhile, combine the ½ cup water and 1 cup of sugar in a saucepan. Bring to a boil. Add the grapefruit peel and boil until all the syrup is absorbed and the peel is transparent. Check the peels often to make sure they don't stick or scorch. Sprinkle a large tray with the additional sugar (1 cup or more). Add the peels and shake until the strips of citrus are well coated. Dry on a wire rack (this will take a day in dry weather, longer if it's humid). Store in airtight containers.

THREE

CHRISTMAS COOKIES

Ginger-Molasses Cutouts *
Christmas Crinkles *
Overnight Snowballs *
Butter Cookies with Cherry Preserves *
Pecan and Date Crescents *
Pushkin's Orange Nut Cookies *
Chocolate and Candied Ginger Lace Cookies *

* A make-ahead recipe

Each of the seven Christmas cookies given here is delicious, dependable and different from most cookie recipes. Even the Butter Cookies with Cherry Preserves are a twist on the popular thumbprint cookies. The Chocolate and Candied Ginger Lace Cookies offer a unique combination of ingredients and are thin, crispy and as lacy as their name implies. Pushkin's Orange Nut Cookies always receive rave reviews and are eaten up about as quickly as they're made. The Ginger-Molasses Cutouts give children a chance to get in on the baking, and the Overnight Snowballs are easy and, since they're left in the oven overnight, are almost no trouble. If you have the time, try them all: they offer a wide variety of tastes and textures and each is well worth the effort.

21

GINGER-MOLASSES CUTOUTS

4 cups flour
1¼ teaspoons ginger
¼ teaspoon grated nutmeg
1 teaspoon cinnamon
1 teaspoon mace
½ teaspoon cloves
¼ cup unsalted butter
¼ cup Crisco
½ cup dark brown sugar, firmly
  packed
1 cup molasses
1½ teaspoon baking soda
1 tablespoon very hot water

Sift together flour and spices. Cream butter, Crisco and sugar until light and fluffy. Add molasses and beat well. Dissolve soda in water. Mix ¼ of dry ingredients into creamed mixture, then stir in soda water. Work in remaining dry ingredients, ⅓ at a time. Wrap dough and chill 6 hours or overnight.

Preheat oven to 350 degrees. Roll dough, a little at a time, using flour on rolling pin and board to keep dough from sticking. Roll the dough to ⅛-inch thickness, the thinner the better. Cut with Christmas cookie cutters and place 1½ inches apart on a lightly greased baking sheet. Bake about 8 minutes. Cool on baking sheet 1 to 2 minutes, then transfer to wire racks to cool. Makes approximately 2 dozen cookies, depending on size of cookie cutters used.

CHRISTMAS CRINKLES

4 ounces unsweetened chocolate,
  melted
½ cup oil
1½ cups sugar
½ cup dark brown sugar
4 eggs
2 teaspoons vanilla
2 cups flour
2 teaspoons baking powder
½ teaspoon salt
¾ cup pecans, finely chopped
  Confectioners' sugar

Mix melted chocolate with the oil and sugars. Add eggs one at a time; then add vanilla. Sift dry ingredients and blend into creamed mixture. Add chopped pecans. Chill for 2 hours. Preheat oven to 350 degrees. Roll dough into balls, and then roll in confectioners' sugar. Place on greased cookie sheets 2 to 3 inches apart. Bake for 10 to 12 minutes. Cool slightly before removing from pan. Makes 4 dozen cookies.

OVERNIGHT SNOWBALLS

2 egg whites
⅔ cup sugar
   pinch of salt
1¼ teaspoons vanilla extract
1 cup pecans, finely chopped
1 cup semisweet chocolate bits

Preheat oven to 350 degrees. Beat egg whites until foamy. Gradually add sugar and continue beating until stiff peaks form. Fold in salt, vanilla, pecans and chocolate bits. Drop cookies by teaspoon onto ungreased, foil-lined baking sheet. Place cookies in preheated oven and immediately turn off the heat. Leave cookies in CLOSED oven overnight. Makes 2 dozen.

BUTTER COOKIES WITH CHERRY PRESERVES

2 cups sifted flour
½ teaspoon salt
1 cup unsalted butter
½ cup sugar
1 teaspoon vanilla extract
1 teaspoon almond extract
   Cherry preserves (approximately ½ cup)

Sift together flour and salt, and set aside. Cream butter and sugar until light and fluffy, then mix in vanilla and almond extracts. Slowly mix in flour, ½ cup at a time, until barely blended. Chill dough for 2 hours.

Preheat oven to 325 degrees. Shape dough into 1-inch balls, handling them quickly, and space 2 inches apart on ungreased baking sheets. Press each ball with thumb to make a deep print. Fill each with a small amount of cherry preserves. Bake for 15 minutes or until lightly colored. Transfer to wire racks to cool. Store in refrigerator, separated by wax paper, in an airtight container. Makes about 4 dozen.

PECAN AND DATE CRESCENTS

½ cup chopped dates
½ cup chopped pecans
½ cup sugar
½ cup light Karo syrup
1 teaspoon water
1 3-ounce package cream cheese, softened
8 tablespoons unsalted butter, softened
1 cup flour

Simmer dates, nuts, sugar, Karo syrup and water, stirring occasionally until thickened. Be careful not to cook to soft ball stage or filling will be too sticky to work with. Cool slightly.

Preheat oven to 350 degrees. Cream together cream cheese and butter; add flour. Place on floured surface. Being sure to use a *floured* rolling pin, roll dough, using flour sparingly to keep dough from sticking. Cut with a 3-inch fluted round cookie cutter. Spread about 1 tablespoon of date/pecan filling on ½ of each cookie. Fold over the other ½, pinching the edges together. Bake in preheated oven for 15 to 20 minutes. Makes about two dozen.

PUSHKIN'S ORANGE NUT COOKIES

2¾ cup sifted flour
½ teaspoon baking soda
½ teaspoon salt
8 tablespoons unsalted butter
½ cup Crisco
½ cup sugar
2 tablespoons orange juice
½ cup dark brown sugar, firmly packed
1 egg
1 teaspoon vanilla extract
1 cup walnuts + ⅓ cup, finely chopped
2 teaspoons grated orange rind + 1 tablespoon

Sift flour with baking soda and salt; set aside. Cream butter and Crisco. Add sugar, orange juice, brown sugar, egg and vanilla, and beat until light and fluffy. At low speed, beat in flour mixture. Add the 1 cup chopped walnuts and 2 teaspoons orange rind. Chill until easy to handle.

Preheat oven to 400 degrees. Form dough into ½-inch balls. Place on ungreased cookie sheet and flatten lightly with hand. Combine the ⅓ cup finely chopped walnuts and 1 tablespoon grated orange rind. Top with a sprinkling of the nut and orange rind mixture. Bake 8 to 10 minutes. Transfer to a wire rack to cool. Makes 3 dozen.

CHOCOLATE AND CANDIED GINGER LACE COOKIES

4 tablespoons unsalted butter, softened
½ cup dark brown sugar, firmly packed
¼ cup sifted flour
¼ cup + 1 tablespoon heavy cream
⅔ cup finely chopped unblanched almonds
⅓ cup minced candied ginger
1 tablespoon grated orange rind
4 ounces bittersweet chocolate (preferably Tobler)
3 tablespoons butter

Preheat oven to 350 degrees. Grease and flour baking sheets. Cream butter and sugar until light and fluffy. Stir in flour alternately with cream. Stir in almonds, candied ginger and orange rind. Drop mixture by teaspoonfuls 3 inches apart on prepared baking sheets. With a knife, spread into 2-inch rounds, keeping cookies as thin and even as possible.

Bake for 12 minutes, until lacey and golden brown. Watch carefully towards the end, as cookies need to brown well but not overcook. Cool on baking sheets 2 minutes, then transfer to wire racks to continue cooling. (If cookies cool too much to easily remove from baking sheets, they can be softened in oven again.)

Melt chocolate and butter together over low heat. Cool slightly and spread flat side of cookies, arranged on wax paper, with a layer of chocolate mixture. When chocolate hardens, store cookies in refrigerator, separated with wax paper, and keep airtight. Makes about 2½ dozen.

FOUR

HOLIDAY DESSERTS

*Christmas Whiskey Cake**
*Three-Tiered Christmas Brownie**
*Wintertime Pumpkin Cheesecake**
*Easy and Delicious Pots de Creme**
*Chocolate Pâté with Raspberry Sauce**
*Cranberry Orange Cake**
*Apple Walnut Cheesecake**
*Chocolate Walnut Torte**

* A make-ahead recipe

That's right, there are no sticky fruitcake recipes here, none of the usual fare you think about at Christmas. But each of the desserts offered here is tried and true and wonderful enough to become a holiday tradition. Whether you prefer something elegant (try the Chocolate Pâté!) or something casual (you'll go for the Three-Tiered Brownie), there's a great dessert here for everyone. The Cranberry Orange Cake and the Whiskey Cake have all the flavors and smells of December, and the Easy and Delicious Pots de Creme are just as their name implies — easy, delicious, the kind of dessert you'll be proud to serve all year. If you want something really different, though, try the Chocolate Walnut Torte (it's made with no flour) or the Pumpkin Cheesecake (it's rich and chock full of good ingredients and lots of spices).

29

CHRISTMAS WHISKEY CAKE

1 cup sugar
1 cup dark brown sugar, firmly
packed
1 cup butter (2 sticks), softened
3 eggs, well beaten
3 cups sifted cake flour
½ teaspoon baking powder
½ teaspoon mace
¾ cup 100 proof bourbon whiskey
¼ cup dark rum
2 cups pecans, chopped

Whiskey Glaze:
½ cup light corn syrup
1 tablespoon dark rum
2 tablespoons bourbon whiskey
Whipped cream

Preheat oven to 250 degrees. Cream together the sugars and butter. Add the eggs. Sift together flour, baking powder and mace; add alternately with the bourbon and rum. Add pecans. Bake in a well greased or paper-lined 9½-inch tube pan. Check after 2 hours and 15 minutes, although it may need to cook an additional 15 to 35 minutes, according to your oven. The cake should have a moist, crumbly texture similar to a macaroon. Wrap in foil and store in a cool place. The cake cuts easier when cold, but should be served at room temperature. It will keep 2 weeks or longer; however, DO NOT FREEZE.

For the glaze, combine the syrup, rum and bourbon and drizzle over each slice of cake just before serving. Spoon on whipped cream.

THREE-TIERED CHRISTMAS BROWNIE

Pastry Layer:
1¾ cup flour
½ cup sugar
½ teaspoon baking powder
¼ teaspoon salt
½ cup butter, cut into pieces and softened
1 egg

Brownie Layer:
½ cup butter
3 tablespoons unsweetened cocoa
1 cup sugar
2 eggs
1 tablespoon cognac
¾ cup flour
½ teaspoon salt

¾ cup strawberry preserves
½ cup pecans, chopped

Preheat oven to 350 degrees. For the pastry layer, combine flour, sugar, baking powder and salt; blend with a fork. Add the softened butter and work into the dry ingredients until the mixture resembles small peas. Add the egg. Combine well, and spread into an ungreased 8-inch pan. Bake for 20 minutes, or until a cake tester comes out clean.

Meanwhile, melt the butter over low heat. Pour into a bowl and add cocoa; stir. Add the sugar. One at a time, add the eggs. Add the cognac, flour and salt, and combine with other ingredients.

To assemble, spread the strawberry preserves over the pastry layer. Then evenly distribute the brownie mixture over the preserves. Sprinkle with pecans. Bake 25 to 30 minutes, or until a tester comes out clean. Cool thoroughly on a wire rack before cutting into squares. Makes 16 brownies.

WINTERTIME PUMPKIN CHEESECAKE

Crust:
- 4 tablespoons butter, melted
- 1¼ cups graham cracker crumbs
- ¼ teaspoon ground cinnamon

Apple-Raisin Filling:
- 4 Granny Smith apples, peeled, cored and chopped
- ½ cup raisins
- ⅔ cup dark brown sugar
- 1 cup dry white wine
- ¼ teaspoon ground cinnamon
- ¼ teaspoon ground cloves
- ½ teaspoon ground ginger
- ½ teaspoon grated nutmeg
- 4 tablespoons butter
- ¼ cup Calvados (apple brandy)

Pumpkin Cheesecake:
- 2½ pounds cream cheese, softened
- ½ cup sugar
- ½ cup dark brown sugar
- 4 eggs
- 3 egg yolks
- 3 tablespoons flour
- 1 teaspoon ground cinnamon
- 1 teaspoon ground ginger
- ¼ teaspoon ground cloves
- ¼ teaspoon grated nutmeg
- 1 cup heavy cream
- 2 teaspoons vanilla extract
- ¼ cup maple syrup
- 2 cups pumpkin puree

Prepare a 10-inch springform pan by wrapping the bottom and sides carefully with aluminum foil (be sure to wrap well so there won't be leaks when cheesecake is baked in the water bath). To make the crust, toss the crumbs and cinnamon with the butter and then press into the bottom of the prepared pan. Chill. Meanwhile, bring to a boil the apples, raisins, brown sugar and wine. Partially cover the saucepan, then lower heat and simmer until apples are tender and liquid is reduced by ½ (about 40 minutes). Add spices, butter and brandy and cook until butter is melted, about 5 minutes more. Cool.

Preheat oven to 425 degrees. While the apple-raisin filling is cooling, beat together the cream cheese, sugars, eggs and yolks until smooth. Add flour, spices, cream, vanilla, maple syrup and pumpkin, and mix thoroughly. Spread a layer of the cooled apple-raisin mixture over the chilled crust. Pour in the cheesecake mixture to fill. Set pan in a larger pan and add hot water to come half way up the sides. Bake in the preheated oven for 15 minutes. Reduce heat to 275 degrees and bake until the filling is set, about another 1½ hours. Remove and let cool. Refrigerate overnight. Bring to room temperature before serving. Serves 12 to 14.

EASY AND DELICIOUS HOLIDAY POTS DE CREME

1 **vanilla bean**
2 **cups half and half**
½ **cup sugar**
6 **egg yolks**
3 **tablespoons white creme de cacao**
   Semisweet chocolate

Preheat oven to 325 degrees. Split vanilla bean down the middle and cut into 1-inch pieces. (Go to the extra trouble to use a vanilla bean; vanilla extract will not provide the same flavor or same results). Scald half and half, sugar and vanilla bean. Cool. Beat egg yolks until thick and lemon-colored. Add half and half, stirring constantly. Add creme de cacao. Strain the mixture through a fine sieve, and pour into six pot de creme cups. Cover each and set in a pan half-filled with water.

Bake in a 325-degree oven for about 30 minutes. Remove from water bath, and cool on a rack. Chill. Serve topped with grated semisweet chocolate. The pots de creme may be made a day ahead of time. Serves 6.

CHOCOLATE PÂTÉ WITH RASPBERRY SAUCE

    5 tablespoons butter
   18 ounces bittersweet chocolate
      (preferably Tobler)
    3 eggs
    2 egg yolks
    1 tablespoon sugar
    2 tablespoons heavy cream
    1 teaspoon vanilla

Raspberry Sauce:
    2 packages frozen raspberries
    ¾ cup red currant jelly
   1½ teaspoons corn starch
    1 tablespoon cold water
    2 tablespoons Framboise

Preheat oven to 425 degrees. Butter and flour a 4-cup loaf pan approximately 7½ by 4 by 2 inches. Butter and flour a piece of parchment paper to fit into the bottom of the pan. In a saucepan, over low heat, melt the butter with the chocolate, stirring until shiny and smooth. Set aside. In a bowl, beat the eggs, yolks and sugar until thickened, about 6 minutes. Stir the cream and vanilla into the egg mixture carefully, then gently fold in the chocolate. Pour into the prepared pan and bake for 20 minutes. Cool completely on a rack, then wrap well and place in freezer.

Before serving, remove pan from freezer and let stand 20 minutes. Unmold chocolate, peeling off parchment paper and let the pâté stand another 20 minutes. (If serving on individual plates, slice the pâté into pieces ⅓-inch thick and place on plates, letting stand 20 minutes.) Slice each piece ⅓-inch thick with a very hot knife. Spoon raspberry sauce around the sides of individual plates.

For the sauce, thaw the berries. Place in a saucepan. Add the jelly and bring the mixture to a boil. Mix the cornstarch with water, and add to the berries. Cook, stirring, until the sauce is clear and thickened slightly. Add the Framboise. Push the sauce through a strainer and cool. (Sauce can be made 2 days in advance and refrigerated until needed.)

CRANBERRY ORANGE CAKE

2¼ cups flour
 ¼ teaspoon salt
 1 teaspoon baking powder
 1 teaspoon baking soda
 1 cup sugar
 1 cup walnuts, chopped
 1 cup dates, diced
 1 cup fresh cranberries, diced
   Rind of 2 oranges, grated
 2 eggs, well beaten
 1 cup buttermilk
 ¾ cup oil

Glaze:
 ¾ cup orange juice
 1 cup sugar
 ¾ cup Grand Marnier

Preheat oven to 350 degrees. Sift together flour, salt, baking powder and soda. Stir in sugar, nuts, dates, cranberries and rind. Combine eggs, milk and oil. Add to the fruit mixture and stir well. Pour into a well-greased 9½-inch tube pan. Bake 50 to 60 minutes. Cool until lukewarm. Remove from pan, and place on a rack with pan underneath. Poke holes in the top of the cake with a toothpick, and pour glaze over the cake; salvage glaze drippings from the pan and pour over again. Serves 12-14.

APPLE WALNUT CHEESECAKE

Crust:
- 1 cup all-purpose flour, sifted
- 1/3 cup granulated sugar
- 8 tablespoons unsalted butter, cut in small pieces and chilled
- 1/4 teaspoon vanilla extract

Cheesecake:
- 1 pound cream cheese, softened
- 1/2 cup granulated sugar
- 2 large eggs, lightly beaten
- 1 teaspoon vanilla extract

Topping:
- 3 medium apples, peeled and sliced
- 1/4 cup granulated sugar
- 1/2 teaspoon ground cinnamon
- 1/8 teaspoon ground nutmeg
- 1/2 teaspoon vanilla extract
- 1/2 cup walnuts, coarsely chopped

For the crust, preheat the oven to 350 degrees. Combine the flour, sugar, butter and vanilla. Mix together with your fingers until the pastry resembles coarse meal. Press the dough into a 9-inch springform pan and bake for 5 minutes. The crust will not be very brown or hard. Set aside to cool.

Preheat the oven to 450 degrees. In a large bowl combine the cream cheese, sugar, eggs and vanilla. Mix until completely blended and pour into the prepared crust. Next, place the apple slices in a large bowl and sprinkle with the sugar, cinnamon, nutmeg and vanilla. Stir to mix well. Layer the apple slices on top of the cheese mixture attractively then sprinkle with the walnuts. Bake for 15 minutes, then reduce the heat to 350 degrees and bake for an additional 45 minutes. Cool to room temperature on a wire rack, then chill. Serves 10 to 12.

CHOCOLATE WALNUT TORTE

Butter
1 9-inch springform pan
8 egg yolks
1 cup sugar
7 ounces bittersweet chocolate,
  melted and cooled
1 teaspoon vanilla
2 cups walnuts, finely ground
8 egg whites
Cream of tartar
Salt
8 ounces semisweet chocolate

Preheat oven to 350 degrees. Generously grease a 9-inch springform pan with butter. Set aside. In a large bowl, beat the egg yolks with the sugar for 5 minutes. Fold in melted bittersweet chocolate, vanilla and walnuts. In another bowl, beat the egg whites with a pinch of cream of tartar and a pinch of salt until the whites hold soft peaks. Stir a fourth of the egg whites into chocolate mixture. Fold in the remaining whites gently but thoroughly. Pour into the springform pan and bake in a 350-degree oven for 45 minutes to 1 hour, or until a cake tester comes out clean. Allow the cake to cool in the pan for 15 minutes, then remove sides of the pan, and invert the cake onto a rack. Cool completely.

For the icing, melt the additional 8 ounces of semi-sweet chocolate. Cool about 5 minutes, then spread over top and sides of the cooled cake with a spatula. Serves 8 to 10.

FIVE

CHRISTMAS OPEN HOUSE

Menu For 20 to 25
Chafing Dish of Scallops and Champagne
Roasted Beef Tender
Belgian Endive with Herbed Cheese
*Pâté with Apples and Brandy**
Platter of Marinated Avocado Balls and
Stuffed Cherry Tomatoes
*Toasted Curried Almonds**
*Christmas Supreme Eggnog**

*Festive Tiny Fruit Cakes**   *Bourbon Brandy Tea Cakes**
Coffee

* *A make-ahead recipe*

Not only are the dishes in this menu wonderful to eat, they also provide a beautiful table for a truly successful open house. Make a wreath with the Stuffed Cherry Tomatoes surrounded by the Marinated Avocado Balls — both of these are great tasting, great looking and a sure step above a platter of cold vegetables. The Pâté with Apples and Brandy is a classic, rich pâté, full of flavor, smooth and delicate. But if you can try only one thing from this menu, let it be Christmas Supreme Eggnog — it's the best you've ever tasted.

CHAFING DISH OF SCALLOPS AND CHAMPAGNE

4 tablespoons butter plus
2 tablespoons
½ cup shallots, diced
1 bay leaf
Salt
Pepper
1½ cups dry champagne
2 pounds scallops, quartered if large, rinsed well and side muscle removed
1 pound mushrooms, sliced
4 tablespoons flour
2 cups creme fraiche (recipe below)
Juice of 1 lemon
1 tablespoon fresh tarragon, chopped
4 tablespoons chives, chopped
2 teaspoons paprika
Cayenne pepper

In a deep skillet melt the first 4 tablespoons butter. Add the shallots, bay leaf, and salt and pepper (to taste, or about ¼ teaspoon each). Over low heat, saute until shallots are golden. Add champagne and the scallops, gently simmering until the scallops are *barely* done. Drain scallops, saving the strained liquid.

In another skillet, saute the mushrooms in additional 2 tablespoons butter, then sprinkle in the flour and stir well, cooking for 2 to 3 minutes. Add the creme fraiche and reserved liquid. Stir until blended well, then add the lemon juice and cook gently until liquid is reduced to desired consistency. Add scallops, tarragon and chives; taste for seasoning. Pour into chafing dish, and sprinkle with paprika and dash of cayenne. Serve with toasted triangles of bread and cocktail picks.

RECIPE FOR CREME FRAICHE:
  1 cup heavy cream
  1 cup sour cream

Blend together and let stand at room temperature, covered with plastic wrap, for 24 hours. Place in refrigerator to thicken. May be made several days in advance.

MAYONNAISE

  1 egg
  1 egg yolk
  ¾ teaspoon salt
  1 teaspoon Dijon mustard
  ½ teaspoon cayenne pepper
  ½ teaspoon pureed onion
  2 cups olive oil
    Juice of 1 lemon

Beat egg and egg yolk. Add seasonings. Slowly add olive oil — drop by drop — beating hard and continuously until it begins to emulsify. Continue adding remaining oil in a slow stream, stirring constantly. Add lemon juice. Stir well, and taste for seasoning. Serve with Roasted Beef Tender. Recipe on next page.

ROASTED BEEF TENDER

**1 8-pound whole beef tenderloin,
trimmed well and weighed again
after trimming (trimmed weight
is necessary to approximate
cooking time)**
4 tablespoons butter, softened
Salt
Pepper

Bring tenderloin to room temperature,
approximately an hour. Preheat oven to
450 degrees. Rub tenderloin with butter.
Place on rack in roasting pan, and sear
in hot oven for 10 minutes. Without
opening door, reduce oven temperature
to 350 degrees, and time exactly 7 minutes to the pound. Remove tenderloin
and cool on a rack. Place a platter underneath rack to collect drippings. Let rest
for 20 minutes. Slice meat very thinly,
and sprinkle with salt and pepper.
Arrange on serving platter and garnish
simply, with watercress or springs of
fresh rosemary. Serve with homemade
Mayonnaise (recipe on previous page)
and Honey-Maple Mustard (see page
15), along with freshly baked rolls or
thin slices of sourdough bread.

(The tenderloin may be roasted up to 2
hours before serving. If so, place back in
same roasting pan, sliced, with accumu-
lated juices. Sprinkle with salt and pepper and gently warm in a 200 degree
oven, just until the chill is removed. It is
important *not* to continue cooking the
tender, simply to warm it.)

BELGIAN ENDIVE WITH HERBED CHEESE

16 ounces cream cheese, softened
2 tablespoons very finely minced green onion, white part only
4 teaspoons finely chopped fresh parsley
¼ teaspoon cayenne pepper
½ teaspoon minced fresh garlic
½ teaspoon salt, or to taste
4 large heads Belgian endive
1 4-ounce jar red salmon caviar

Combine cream cheese, minced onion, parsley, cayenne, minced garlic, and salt in a small bowl; mix until well blended. Set aside. With a sharp knife, cut off (and discard) the bottom ends of the endive. Separate the leaves, wash and dry thoroughly. Use the smaller leaves and, if needed, cut the larger ones in half lengthwise.

Place a fourth of the cream cheese mixture at a time in a pastry bag. Using a back-and-forth movement, pipe the seasoned cheese down the center of each endive leaf. Transfer the caviar eggs from the jar, spacing several of them evenly atop the herbed cheese. Refrigerate until ready to serve. (The herbed cheese mixture can be made the day before; cover and refrigerate, then bring to room temperature and pipe into endive leaves an hour or 2 before the party.) Arrange attractively on a serving platter. Makes approximately 50.

PÂTÉ WITH APPLES AND BRANDY

1 pound chicken livers

16 tablespoons butter, softened and cut into 16 equal pieces

½ cup yellow onions, chopped

¼ cup tart apple, peeled, pared and chopped

2 tablespoons shallots, chopped

¼ cup brandy

3 tablespoons cream

1 teaspoon lemon juice

1 teaspoon salt

¼ teaspoon black pepper, freshly ground

½ pound butter, clarified

Wash and dry chicken livers, and cut in half. Melt 3 tablespoons of butter in a skillet and saute the onion for 5 minutes. Add apples and shallots and cook 2 minutes more. Place the mixture in a food processor and blend thoroughly.

Meanwhile, melt 3 tablespoons butter in same skillet and brown livers, stirring for 3 to 4 minutes on a high heat. Add brandy and cook 2 minutes longer. Add livers and juice to other ingredients in the food processor and blend. Add cream and blend rapidly, until very smooth. Place the pâté in a bowl and cool to room temperature. When cool, add remaining 10 tablespoons butter, along with the lemon juice, salt and pepper. Mix thoroughly and ladle into an attractive silver or crystal bowl. Pour clarified butter over the top, covering well to form a good seal. Chill 2 hours or longer. Allow pâté to reach room temperature before serving. Serve with crackers of thinly sliced French bread. (The pâté freezes well and can be made ahead.)

STUFFED CHERRY TOMATOES

25 medium cherry tomatoes
   Salt
   Pepper
16 ounces cream cheese, softened
 8 strips bacon, cooked, drained and
   finely crumbled
 1 4½ ounce can ripe olives,
   chopped
 1 tablespoon finely grated onion
   Cayenne Pepper
   Finely chopped fresh herbs

Slice in half cherry tomatoes. Scoop out pulp with melon ball scooper. Sprinkle with salt and pepper, then turn upside down on paper towels to drain. Meanwhile, combine the softened cream cheese, crumbled bacon, olives, grated onion and pepper. Taste for seasoning. (The cream cheese mixture may be made a day or two ahead of time, then returned to room temperature before continuing recipe.) With a small spoon, stuff tomato halves with the cream cheese mixture. Cover with plastic wrap and refrigerate until ready to use. Before serving, sprinkle with finely chopped herbs, such as chives, basil or parsley. Serve on tray surrounded by avocado balls. Makes 50.

MARINATED AVOCADO BALLS

6 large avocados
  Lemon juice
1 teaspoon coarse (kosher) salt
1 teaspoon freshly ground black
  pepper
2 tablespoons fresh chives, chopped
1 teaspoon Dijon mustard
4 tablespoons red wine vinegar
10 tablespoons olive oil
6 tablespoons vegetable oil

Cut avocados in half, and remove seeds. With a melon ball scooper, scoop balls from the avocado pulp. (Each ball may not be perfectly round.) Roll balls in lemon juice to prevent discoloration. In a small bowl, combine the salt, pepper, chives, mustard and red wine vinegar. Stir well with a fork or whisk. Slowly pour in the olive oil and vegetable oil, stirring constantly to mix well. Taste, and add more oil, vinegar or seasonings if needed. Pour the vinaigrette over the avocado balls, cover and refrigerate. When ready to use, drain and place rounded side up on a large platter around the stuffed cherry tomatoes. Serve avocado balls with cocktail picks.

TOASTED CURRIED ALMONDS

3 teaspoons salt (or to taste)
3 teaspoons curry powder
6 cups whole blanched almonds
6 tablespoons butter, melted
3 tablespoons curry powder
1 teaspoon Worcestershire
¼ teaspoon Tabasco

Preheat oven to 300 degrees. Combine the salt and the 3 teaspoons curry powder in a small bowl; set aside.

Mix together the remaining 5 ingredients and spread out on cake pans. Toast in batches in preheated oven for 30 to 45 minutes, stirring occasionally, until golden. Drain the almonds on paper towels and when cool, sprinkle with the curry-salt mixture, tossing well to cover. (Toasted Curried Almonds freeze well, and may be made ahead of time.) Store in airtight containers. Makes approximately 6 cups.

CHRISTMAS SUPREME EGGNOG

8 egg yolks
½ to ¾ cup sugar
1½ cups bourbon whiskey
1 teaspoon vanilla extract
8 egg whites
   pinch of salt
2 cups whipping cream

Whip yolks till lemon-colored and light. Gradually, while beating, add sugar and then bourbon and vanilla. (The recipe can be refrigerated at this point and the other ingredients added later.)

Whip the egg whites with a pinch of salt until peaks form. In a chilled bowl, with chilled beaters or whisk, whip the cream until soft peaks form. Fold the whites and cream into the yolk and bourbon mixture. Thin with a small amount of milk, if desired. Refrigerate. (Supreme Eggnog can be made in the late afternoon for a party the same night.) This recipe serves 12 to 15; you will need to double the quantities for the Christmas Open House, but make the recipe in 2 batches for easier handling and mixing.

FESTIVE TINY FRUIT CAKES

½ cup butter
1 cup sugar
2 eggs
2 cups flour, sifted
1 teaspoon baking soda
1 cup dates, chopped
1 cup walnuts, chopped
⅔ cup buttermilk
1 tablespoon grated orange rind
1 teaspoon grated lemon rind

Topping:
¾ cup sugar
½ cup orange juice
1 tablespoon grated orange rind

Preheat oven to 375. Cream butter and sugar until light. Add eggs, one at a time. Sift dry ingredients together, then add dates and nuts. Alternate dry mixture with buttermilk in adding to egg mixture. Blend in orange and lemon rind. Grease miniature muffin tins and fill ⅔ full. Bake for 10-15 minutes.

Meanwhile, combine sugar, orange juice and rind in a sauce pan. Bring to boil. Pour slowly over the cakes while they are still hot. Makes 5 dozen.

BOURBON BRANDY TEA CAKES

2 cups finely ground almonds
½ cup fine breadcrumbs
¾ cup golden raisins
6 eggs, separated
¾ cup firmly packed light-brown sugar, free of lumps plus ¼ cup (also free of lumps)
⅓ cup bourbon
3 tablespoons brandy
Confectioners' sugar

Preheat oven to 375 degrees. Combine almonds, breadcrumbs and raisins. In a separate bowl, beat together egg yolks and the ¾ cup brown sugar until the mixture is thick and light colored. Set aside.

Beat egg whites until foamy, gradually adding the remaining ¼ cup brown sugar. Continue beating until soft peaks form. Alternately fold egg whites and nut/raisin mixture into the egg yolk mixture. Stir in bourbon and brandy.

Spoon mixture into well-buttered tiny muffin tins. Bake for 10 minutes. Cool and dust lightly with confectioners' sugar. (The Tea Cakes can be made ahead; keep in refrigerator in plastic bags after thoroughly cooling. Bring to room temperature before serving.) Makes 60.

SIX

CHRISTMAS EVE SUPPER
Menu for 8

*Macadamia Cheddar Snaps** *(page 4)*
*Christmas Supreme Eggnog** *(page 48)*
*Hot Spiced Cider**

*Fireside Pork Stew**
Green Salad with Vinaigrette
French Bread

*Chocolate Walnut Torte** *(page 37)*
Coffee

*A make-ahead recipe

This is the kind of meal of which memories are made. From the moment guests come through the front door or family members pile through the back door, they'll be welcomed by the cinnamony smells of Hot Spiced Cider and a basket full of Macadamia Cheddar Snaps. And the Fireside Pork Stew, full of more great tastes and smells, is a hearty, comforting dish no one will forget — especially when it's combined with a crisp green salad, crusty French bread and a glass of wine. To top it off, give everyone a slice of Chocolate Walnut Torte and a steaming cup of black coffee. Waiting for St. Nick will never have been so much fun.

HOT SPICED CIDER

2 quarts apple cider
3 cinnamon sticks
2 teaspoons freshly grated nutmeg
2 teaspoons whole cloves
¼ teaspoon ground allspice
1 tablespoon honey
½ cup fresh lemon juice
2 cups fresh orange juice
2 strips orange peel, orange part only

Boil the cider and spices together for fifteen minutes. Add the honey, lemon and orange juices and orange peel. Simmer, and serve warm. This hot beverage makes the whole house smell like Christmas and is particularly welcoming for those coming in from the cold outdoors. It's also a nice alternative to alcoholic drinks and a festive drink for teenagers and children on Christmas Eve. (The spiced cider may be made ahead of time and reheated.)

FIRESIDE PORK STEW

4½ pounds boneless pork shoulder,
    trimmed and cut into 1½-inch
    cubes
    Salt
    Freshly ground black pepper
4 tablespoons vegetable oil
3 tablespoons unsalted butter
2 garlic cloves, peeled and minced
2 medium onions, chopped
2¾ cups apple cider
2 strips lemon peel, each stuck
    with 2 whole cloves
2 bay leaves
½ teaspoon dried sage
2¾ cups chicken stock
1 cup pitted prunes
3 large very firm pears, peeled,
    cored, and cut into ½-inch slices

(*Note: This recipe can be time consuming because of having to cut up the pork shoulder. But the preparation, and most of the cooking, can be completed the day before. The smells and taste of this dish are well worth the effort).

Season the pork with salt and pepper and cook it in batches in 1 tablespoon oil and 1 tablespoon butter in a large skillet over medium-high heat, turning it, until browned, adding more oil as necessary. Transfer to a large pot when browned. Cook the garlic and onion in the skillet over low heat, stirring, until softened (about 5 minutes), adding more oil as necessary to prevent sticking. Add the cider and bring to a boil, scraping up the brown bits. Add the mixture to the pork with the clove-studded lemon peel, bay leaf, sage and enough stock just to cover the pork. Bring the mixture to the boil and simmer, covered, for 50 minutes. (The stew may be prepared up to this point the day before; the next day, bring mixture to a simmer before continuing recipe.) Add the prunes and simmer the mixture until the pork is tender, about 10 minutes.

Remove the pork and prunes with a slotted spoon to a large dish and set aside, covered. Discard the bay leaf and lemon peel. Skim the fat from the cooking liquid and boil until reduced to 1½ cups, about 20 to 25 minutes. Meanwhile, saute the pear slices in the remaining 1 tablespoon butter in a skillet over medium-high heat until lightly browned, about 3 minutes. (Make sure the pears are very firm so they do not fall apart.) Add to the pork and prunes and top with the sauce. Serves 8.

VINAIGRETTE

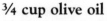

¾ cup olive oil
¼ cup wine vinegar
¼ teaspoon Worcestershire
 1 clove garlic, cut in half
 1 teaspoon sugar
½ teaspoon salt
¼ teaspoon paprika
¼ teaspoon dry mustard
⅛ teaspoon black pepper
⅛ teaspoon thyme

Combine all ingredients and refrigerate. Remove garlic, and shake well. Toss thoroughly with crisp, dry greens such as endive, green leaf lettuce, parsley and watercress.

SEVEN

CHRISTMAS DINNER
Menu for 8

*Oyster Spinach Bisque**

Standing Rib Roast with Mustard Sauce
*Broccoli Wreath with Roasted Red Peppers**
Wild Rice with Pecans
Julienned Parsnips and Carrots
Orange Muffins

*Maple Syrup Mousse with Sugared Walnuts**

*Chocolate Orange Truffles** (page 16)
Coffee

*A make-ahead recipe

This dinner is elegant and celebrative, the perfect climax to the most special holiday of the year. The standing rib roast and seafood offer an alternative to the traditional — and worn out — turkey and ham. Although this menu requires a good deal of preparation, several of the recipes can be made the day (or several days) ahead of time and the rest of the meal assembled Christmas Day.

OYSTER SPINACH BISQUE

3 12-ounce containers of select
  oysters
1 large onion, chopped
1 cup celery, chopped
2 medium leeks (white part only),
  chopped
3 cloves garlic, finely chopped
8 tablespoons unsalted butter
¼ cup flour
⅔ cup dry white wine
1½ to 2 pounds spinach, blanched,
  drained, and dried
4½ cups heavy cream
  Salt
  Black pepper, freshly ground
  Cayenne pepper
  Nutmeg, freshly ground

Reserve liquor from oysters, and set aside. Saute in a large pot the onion, celery, leeks and garlic in the butter until soft (approximately 10 minutes). Add flour, and continue cooking on medium to low heat, stirring, for about 3 minutes. Gradually add wine and ¾ to 1 cup oyster liquor. Bring to a boil.

Add the spinach, stirring frequently to prevent scorching. Add oysters with remaining liquor and cook over medium heat until edges curl (4 to 5 minutes). Remove from the heat and pour into a food processor, with the metal blade in place. Process, but stopping before the mixture is entirely smooth. Pour the contents into a double boiler, add the cream and heat. Season to taste with salt, peppers and ground nutmeg, being sure to add enough salt. (The bisque can be made the day before and gently reheated, stirring constantly, before serving; check again for seasoning.) Ladle into small soup bowls, and garnish with another sprinkling of nutmeg. Serves 8.

STANDING RIB ROAST WITH MUSTARD SAUCE

1 6-pound rib roast (with bone)
Salt
Pepper

Heat oven and roasting pan to 500 degrees. Season the roast with salt and pepper. Place rib roast in pan and sear at 500 degrees for 10 minutes. Lower heat to 350 and roast until internal temperature registers 125 degrees on a meat thermometer (approximately 90 minutes more, or at approximately 17 minutes per pound, total cooking time). After removing from oven, let roast rest for about 20 minutes; while roast rests, make sauce (see below). Carve roast and serve with Mustard Sauce. Serves 8.

Mustard Sauce:
  ½ cup dry white wine
  4 tablespoons prepared yellow mustard
  4 tablespoons Dijon mustard
  4 tablespoons coarse grain mustard
  2 cups heavy cream

Degrease drippings; then deglaze pan by boiling the white wine for about 1 minute, scraping bits from the bottom of the pan with a wooden spoon while the wine boils. Combine mustards and add to wine; bring to a simmer. Add the cream and continue simmering, stirring occasionally, until sauce has been reduced and thickened to desired consistency, approximately 15 to 20 minutes.

BROCCOLI WREATH WITH ROASTED RED PEPPERS

Softened butter for mold
1 large bunch fresh broccoli (about 1½ pounds)
4 tablespoons unsalted butter
1 medium onion, chopped
2 shallots, minced
¼ cup chopped parsley
1 clove garlic, minced
1½ cups milk
1 cup bread crumbs
7 eggs
½ cup grated Jarlsberg cheese
½ cup grated Parmesan cheese
Salt, pepper, nutmeg to taste
Boiling water

Butter a 6-cup ring mold, and line the bottom with wax paper. Butter the paper and set aside mold. Steam broccoli for 3 to 4 minutes, just until bright green color appears. Refresh with cold water, then dry well on paper towels. Chop finely. Melt the 4 tablespoons butter in a skillet and sauté the onion and shallots just until soft; do not let them color. Add parsley, garlic and chopped broccoli, and cook over low heat about 5 minutes. In a large bowl, combine the milk and breadcrumbs, then beat in the eggs slowly. Add the broccoli mixture, stirring constantly. Stir in cheeses, and add salt, pepper and nutmeg; taste for seasoning. Pour into prepared ring mold. (The mold can be refrigerated at this point for several hours or overnight.)

Preheat oven to 325 degrees. Place the ring mold inside a larger ovenproof pan. Pour enough boiling water in the pan to come ⅓ of the way up the sides of the mold. Bake about 45 minutes or until the mixture is firm, being careful not to overcook. (If broccoli mold is not served immediately, it may sit in the water bath

— out of the oven — to remain warm.) To serve, unmold ring, peeling off wax paper, and place strips of roasted red pepper over the top of the broccoli in a slightly sloping pattern.

ROASTED RED PEPPERS

2 **large red bell peppers**
  Olive oil
  Salt
  Black pepper

Place red peppers on a baking sheet and put directly under broiler to blacken. Turn when necessary to blacken evenly. (This can also be done by holding a pepper over a gas flame.) When all sides are charred, place in a bowl and cover tightly with plastic wrap; leave in the covered bowl for about 10 minutes to steam. Remove pepper from bowl and carefully peel off skin. Remove the inner core and all seeds. Slice the peppers in ½-inch wide strips. Season with a little olive oil, salt and pepper. (Peppers can be roasted two days before using and refrigerated in an airtight container; heat gently to remove chill before serving.)

WILD RICE WITH PECANS

1½ cups wild rice
4 tablespoons vegetable oil
⅓ cup shallots, diced
⅓ cup carrots, diced
5 cups chicken stock
4 bay leaves
¼ teaspoon black pepper
3 tablespoons unsalted butter
¾ cup pecan halves
Salt, to taste

In a strainer rinse well the wild rice; shake well to dry. Preheat the oven to 325 degrees. Heat the vegetable oil in a heavy saucepan. Add the wild rice, shallots and carrots and sauté over medium heat, stirring constantly, for 5 minutes. Add the chicken stock, bay leaves and black pepper, and bring to a boil. Transfer to an ovenproof casserole. Tightly cover, and place in preheated oven; cook for 1½ to 2 hours, or until the rice is tender and has absorbed the liquid. Stir occasionally, and add a small amount of water if the rice is beginning to dry out before it's tender.

Melt the 3 tablespoons butter, and sauté the pecan halves over low heat. Add to the rice, and mix gently. Check for seasoning, adding salt if necessary. Serves 8.

JULIENNED PARSNIPS AND CARROTS

3 cups chicken stock
8 carrots, cut in thin 3-inch
   julienned strips
8 parsnips, cut in thin 3-inch
   julienned strips
2 tablespoons brown sugar
½ cup fresh orange juice
6 tablespoons butter, chilled
   Salt
   Pepper

Bring chicken stock to a simmer. Cook the carrots in the stock until tender crisp, about 5 minutes. Remove with a slotted spoon, and cook the parsnips in the same stock until tender, about 3 minutes. Remove parsnips. Add brown sugar to the stock, and boil to reduce to ⅓ cup, about 25 minutes. Add orange juice, and simmer for another 10 minutes. Swirl in the butter. Stir in carrots and parsnips, and season to taste with salt and pepper.

ORANGE MUFFINS

2 cups flour
1 tablespoon baking powder
½ cup sugar
¾ teaspoon salt
5 tablespoons Crisco
2 tablespoons grated orange rind
1 egg, well beaten
½ cup orange juice

Sift dry ingredients together. Cut in shortening. Add orange rind. Combine the beaten egg and orange juice, and add to the flour mixture, stirring only until flour is moist. Fill greased muffin tins ⅔ full. Bake 15 to 20 at 425 degrees.

MAPLE MOUSSE WITH SUGARED WALNUTS

1 cup maple syrup
3 large eggs, separated and at room
  temperature
  pinch cream of tartar
  pinch salt
2 cups heavy cream, well chilled
  Brown Sugar Walnuts, chopped
  (see page 12)

Boil the maple syrup in a large, heavy saucepan over medium-high heat for 3 minutes, swirling the pan gently several times. Cool for 3 minutes. Process the egg yolks in a food processor for approximately 3 minutes. With the motor running, add the syrup in a slow, steady stream through the feed tube. Transfer to a large bowl and cool for 20 minutes.

Beat the egg whites, cream of tartar and salt until soft peaks form. Set aside. In a chilled bowl, beat the cream with an electric mixer until soft peaks form. Fold cream into the egg whites; fold into the maple syrup mixture gently but thoroughly. Divide the mousse among 8 dessert dishes and freeze until just firm, about 1 hour. (The mousse may be frozen longer and softened at room temperature for 15 to 20 minutes before serving.) Top with chopped Brown Sugar Walnuts (page 12). Serves 8.

Index

A

Apples:
    apple walnut cheese cake, 36
    pâté with apples and brandy, 44
    wintertime pumpkin cheesecake, 32
Apple Walnut Cheesecake, 36
Appetizers: see Hors D'Oeuvres

B

Beef:
    honey raisin meatballs in chafing dish, 5
    roasted beef tender, 42
    standing rib roast with mustard sauce, 57
Belgian Endive with Herbed Cheese, 43
Beverages:
    Christmas supreme eggnog, 48
    hot spiced cider, 52
Bourbon Brandy Tea Cakes, 50
Brandy:
    bourbon brandy tea cakes, 50
    pâté with apples and brandy, 44
Broccoli Wreath with Roasted Red Peppers, 58
Brown Sugar Walnuts, 12
Brownies:
    three-tiered Christmas brownie, 31
Butter Cookies with Cherry Preserves, 25

C

Cakes:
    chocolate walnut torte, 37
    Christmas whiskey cake, 30
    cranberry orange cake, 35

Candied Grapefruit Peel, 19
Chafing Dish of Scallops and Champagne, 40
Cheese:
    Belgian endive with herbed cheese, 43
    chutney almond cheese mold, 2
    macadamia cheddar snaps, 4
Cheesecakes:
    apple walnut cheesecake, 36
    wintertime pumpkin cheesecake, 32
Chicken:
    curried chicken on bibb boats, 6
Chocolate:
    chocolate and candied ginger lace cookies, 28
    chocolate orange truffles, 16
    chocolate pâté with raspberry sauce, 34
    Christmas crinkles, 23
    Christopher's Christmas chocolate sauce, 13
    rum-flavored chocolate truffles, 17
    three-tiered Christmas brownie, 31
Chocolate and Candied Ginger Lace Cookies, 28
Chocolate Orange Truffles, 16
Chocolate Pâté with Raspberry Sauce, 34
Chocolate Walnut Torte, 37
Christmas Supreme Eggnog, 48
Christmas Whiskey Cake, 30
Christopher's Christmas Chocolate Sauce, 13
Chutney Almond Cheese Mold, 2
Cookies:
    butter cookies with cherry preserves, 25
    chocolate and candied ginger lace cookies, 28
    Christmas crinkles, 23

giant coconut chippers, 18
ginger-molasses cutouts, 22
overnight snowballs, 24
pecan and date crescents, 26
Pushkin's orange nut cookies, 27
Crab Mousse, 3
Cranberry Orange Cake, 35
Curried Chicken on Bibb Boats, 6

D
Desserts:
apple walnut cheesecake, 36
bourbon brandy tea cakes, 50
chocolate walnut torte, 37
chocolate pâté with raspberry sauce, 34
cranberry orange cake, 35
Christmas whiskey cake, 30
easy and delicious pots de creme, 33
festive tiny fruit cakes, 49
maple syrup mousse with sugared walnut
topping, 63
three-tiered Christmas brownie, 31
wintertime pumpkin cheesecake, 32
Dressings:
marinade,
for avocado balls, 46
mayonnaise, 41
raspberry guava sauce, 14
vinaigrette, 54

E
Easy and Delicious Pots de Creme, 33

F
Festive Tiny Fruit Cakes, 49
Fireside Pork Stew, 53
Fruit:

apple walnut cheesecake, 36
candied grapefruit peel, 19
cranberry orange cake, 35
festive tiny fruit cakes, 49
fireside pork stew, with pears, 53
pâté with apples and brandy, 44
raspberry sauce, for chocolate pâté, 34
wintertime pumpkin cheesecake, 32

G
Giant Coconut Chippers, 18
Gifts:
brown sugar walnuts, 12
candied grapefruit peel, 19
chocolate orange truffles, 16
Christopher's Christmas chocolate sauce, 13
giant coconut chippers, 18
honey-maple mustard, 15
raspberry guava sauce, 14
rum-flavored chocolate truffles, 17
salted pecans, 12
sweet horseradish mustard, 15
toasted curried almonds, 47
Ginger:
ginger molasses cutouts, 22
chocolate and candied ginger lace cookies, 28
Ginger-Molasses Cutouts, 22
Green Salad with Vinaigrette, 54

H
Ham:
maple-butter ham canapes, 7
Honey-Maple Mustard, 15
Honey Raisin Meatballs in Chafing Dish, 5
Hors D'Oeuvres:
Belgian endive with herbed cheese, 43

chafing dish of scallops and champagne, 40
chutney almond cheese mold, 2
crab mousse, 3
curried chicken on bibb boats, 6
honey raisin meatballs in chafing dish, 5
hot olive onion triangles, 4
hot spicy oysters on croutons, 9
macadamia cheddar snaps, 4
maple-butter ham canapes, 7
marinated avocado balls, 46
pâté with apples and brandy, 44
salted pecans, 12
shrimp mousse, 8
stuffed cherry tomatoes, 45
toasted curried almonds, 47
Hot Olive Onion Triangles, 4
Hot Spiced Cider, 52
Hot Spicy Oysters on Croutons, 9

J
Julienned Parsnips and Carrots, 61

M
Macadamia Cheddar Snaps, 4
Maple-Butter Ham Canapes, 7
Maple Mousse with Sugared
  Walnuts, 63
Marinated Avocado Balls, 46
Mayonnaise, 41
Mustard:
  honey-maple mustard, 15
  mustard sauce,
    for standing rib roast, 57
  sweet horseradish mustard, 15

N
Nuts:
  apple walnut cheesecake, 36
  brown sugar walnuts, 12
  chocolate walnut torte, 37
  chutney almond cheese mold, 2
  macadamia cheddar snaps, 4
  pecan and date crescents, 26
  pecans and wild rice, 60
  salted pecans, 12
  toasted curried almonds, 47

O
Orange:
  cranberry orange cake, 35
  festive tiny fruit cakes, 49
  orange muffins, 62
  Pushkin's orange nut cookies, 27
Orange Muffins, 62
Overnight Snowballs, 24
Oyster Spinach Bisque, 56

P
Pâté:
  chocolate pâté with raspberry sauce, 34
  pâté with apples and brandy, 44
Pecan and Date Crescents, 26
Pork:
  fireside pork stew, 53
  maple-butter ham canapes, 7
Pumpkin:
  wintertime pumpkin cheesecake, 32
Pushkin's Orange Nut Cookies, 27

R
Raspberry Guava Sauce, 14
Rice:
    wild rice with pecans, 60
Roasted Beef Tender, 42
Roasted Red Peppers, 59
Rum-flavored Chocolate Truffles, 17

S
Salted Pecans, 12
Sauces:
    Christopher's Christmas chocolate sauce, 13
    mayonnaise, 41
    mustard sauce,
        for standing rib roast, 57
    raspberry guava sauce, 14
    vinaigrette, 54
Seafood:
    chafing dish of scallops and champagne, 40
    crab mousse, 3
    hot spicy oysters on croutons, 9
    oyster spinach bisque, 56
    shrimp mousse, 8
Shrimp Mousse, 8
Standing Rib Roast with Mustard Sauce, 57
Stuffed Cherry Tomatoes, 45

T
Three-Tiered Christmas Brownie, 31
Toasted Curried Almonds, 47
Tomatoes:
    stuffed cherry tomatoes, 45

V
Vegetables:
    Belgian endive with herbed cheese, 43
    broccoli wreath with roasted red peppers, 58
    carrots,
        julienned with parsnips, 61
    parsnips,
        julienned with carrots, 61
    red peppers,
        roasted, 59
Vinaigrette, for green salad, 54

W
Walnuts:
    apple walnut cheesecake, 36
    brown sugar walnuts, 12
    chocolate walnut torte, 37
Wild Rice with Pecans, 60
Wintertime Pumpkin Cheesecake, 32